MW01469240

For GOD, GLORY, *and* GOLD

For GOD, GLORY, *and* GOLD

Spanish Exploration of *La Florida* and the Mainland:
1513-1543

James E. MacDougald

Marsden House

FOR GOD, GLORY, AND GOLD
Spanish Exploration of *La Florida* and the Mainland:1513-1543

Published by Marsden House
St. Petersburg, Florida

Copyright © 2024 by James E. MacDougald

Cover: Early 16th-Century Spanish Comb Morion helmet. Often called a "Conquistador" helmet. Gifted by the author to the St. Petersburg Museum of History.

Library of Congress Control Number: 2024937821

ISBN (paperback): 9781662951893
ISBN (hardcover): 9781662953637
eISBN: 9781662953620

Preface

The last section of this book contains seven maps. Six of the maps are color prints of the maps that were created by J.G. Kohl to provide with his book, *The Two Oldest General Maps of America Issued in 1527 and 1529* (translated from German), published in 1860. Kohl copied the North and South America portions of the original Spanish world maps in the collection of the Grand Ducal Library in Weimar, Germany. The two-foot by three-foot maps were folded and inserted into a slot inside the back cover. The book was recently acquired by the author. The maps were scanned at high resolution and sections enlarged, resulting in the first-ever publication of select areas of the maps, showing place names of areas along the Gulf Coast and Florida.

The seventh map was created by the author. It is based on places visited and described by Álvar Núñez Cabeza de Vaca in his *Relación*, recounting the landing place of the 1528 Narváez Expedition, and by Rodrigo Rangel, the private secretary of Hernando de Soto, who described the landing place of the later 1539 De Soto Expedition. The identification of Safety Harbor as the site of the 1521 settlement by Juan Ponce de León is explained in the text accompanying the map.

The New World

Christopher Columbus's discovery of "the Indies" in 1492 launched a frantic effort by rich and powerful men intent on claiming, for the king and for themselves, as much territory as possible in what was to become known as the New World.

Columbus, who had secured the titles of Viceroy and Admiral of the Ocean Sea, followed his first expedition with three more. He brought more than 1,700 settlers to the island of Hispaniola, where he established the capital of the Indies in Santo Domingo in what is now the Dominican Republic. From 1492 until 1503 ships launched from various ports in Spain and the islands of the Indies, each hopeful of gaining their riches, perhaps from the import of spices, silver, and gold, or from the establishment of mines and plantations in this strange new world. To gain additional control, Queen Isabella established the *Casa de Contratación* (House of Contracts) in 1503, requiring all ships traveling to or from Spain and the Indies to first achieve permission from the crown. All trips to the New World must be authorized in advance, begin and end in Seville, report all of its travels including maps and latitudes, and acknowledge that all lands discovered were the property of the crown and that 20 percent of all riches acquired must be remitted to the king and queen (the "King's Fifth"). In 1508, the crown added to its duties, requiring that all captains and pilots of ships traveling to the Indies must have certified navigational instruments, trained pilots, and official maps produced by the crown's officially appointed pilots and cosmographers at the *Casa de Contratación*. They also appointed a high court, the *Audiencia*, in Santo Domingo in 1511, which was responsible for assuring that the laws of the crown were obeyed.

Christopher Columbus had been stripped of his titles in 1500 because of his tyrannical rule. He died in 1506, at which time his son, Diego, began a multi-year quest to obtain the title of Viceroy of the Indies for himself. Finally, in 1512, he won his appeal and was named Viceroy of all the lands that his father had discovered which included the islands of Hispaniola, Cuba, Jamaica, and Puerto Rico. Importantly, Columbus had never discovered the North American continent. Our story begins with the "discovery" of *La Florida* in 1513.

The Discovery of La Florida

Juan Ponce de León became the discoverer and governor of *La Florida* in a most unusual way. He had come to the Indies on Columbus's second voyage in 1493. He later conquered Puerto Rico in 1508 and subsequently became its governor, where he built an empire of estates. In 1506, Christopher Columbus died, and his son, Diego, undertook a long legal quest to obtain the title of Viceroy for himself. He won, becoming the Viceroy of the Indies in 1512, but only of the islands that his father had discovered. He immediately removed Ponce de León as the governor of Puerto Rico. Ponce de León went to Spain and complained of the unfairness to his friend, King Ferdinand. The king offered him a consolation prize, allowing him to "discover" whatever he could find north of the known islands in the Indies. Once claiming the island, the king would appoint him as its governor, independent of Viceroy Diego Columbus. They both knew that at least one island, *Binini*, existed, and there might be others, too. Ponce de León accepted the deal and returned to Puerto Rico, sailing to discover new lands in 1513.

The common belief that Juan Ponce de León sailed blindly from Puerto Rico and "discovered" *La Florida* is an inaccurate one. Ponce de

León had lived in the Indies for twenty years and knew the islands of the Indies very well. He had become a rich and powerful man and he certainly knew the pilots and captains of many ships that visited Puerto Rico in their travels around the Indies, some of which probably worked directly for him. There is no doubt that he knew where to go to find at least one "officially undiscovered" island, which was north of Cuba and west of the Bahamas.

Juan Ponce de León launched his three-ship expedition in March 1513 and "discovered" and named *La Florida* on Easter Sunday, landing on its east coast near present-day St. Augustine. He then sailed south around the tip of Florida and north along the Gulf Coast. On his landing in southwestern Florida, he was immediately met by the hostile and treacherous Calusa. Undoubtedly, the Calusa were anxious to repel Spaniards because unauthorized "slavers" had visited before. In his attempts to negotiate with the chief of the Calusa, he used the services of a local Indian who spoke Spanish, which he had learned as a slave before escaping back to South Florida. The peace attempt failed. Juan Ponce's men were attacked by eighty Indian archers in canoes, leading Juan Ponce to determine that it was time to leave. He sailed southward to find "Binini" or any other island, but all he found was a barren island with many turtles. He named it Tortugas and returned to Puerto Rico.

Ponce de León returned to Spain in 1514 to report his great discovery of *La Florida* to the king. He *was* knighted, feted for his great accomplishment, and appointed its *adelantado* by the king. Juan Ponce had seen nothing of great interest in *La Florida* and returned to his estate in Puerto Rico. A year later King Ferdinand died, replaced by his sixteen-year-old grandson, Carlos I. Ponce de León immediately returned to Spain to protect his interests in *La Florida*, staying there for two and a half years. While in Spain from 1516 to 1518, Juan Ponce learned that the adelantado of Cuba, Diego Velázquez de Cuéllar, was sending ships and men to poach and enslave the Indians in *La Florida*. He got the king to issue a royal decree (*cédula*) telling Velázquez to stop. He would also learn that an expedition returning to Cuba from Mexico in 1517 had been forced by prevailing winds to stop in *La Florida* at the same place that Ponce de León landed in 1513. The landing was a disaster. The Calusa had attacked, killing some and wounding many, including its leader, Francisco Hernández de Córdoba, who died of his wounds when the ships returned to Cuba. Finally, in May 1518, Ponce de León returned to Puerto Rico from Spain, his position as adelantado having been affirmed by the new king.

There is no record of Ponce de León returning to Florida in 1519 or 1520, although he would certainly have sent ships and men to map his island and identify good places for a settlement and it is possible that he personally joined some of them. It may be at this time that the legend that Ponce de León was searching for the "Fountain of Youth" began. It is more likely that he was fixated on trying to determine where fountains of fresh water existed that could support a settlement. He would also seek arable land to support livestock and crops. He certainly would not have chosen to try to settle lands controlled by the extremely hostile Calusa in the Charlotte Harbor area.

It is inconceivable that Juan Ponce or his men would not have found Tampa Bay. It is the largest and only deep-water bay on the west coast of Florida. Juan Ponce's men would have been looking for four things: accessibility by large ships, fresh water in large amounts, arable lands, and Indians who were not Calusa, who could be bartered with, accepting trinkets in return for tolerating a settlement nearby. Tampa Bay had all of those, including freshwater springs near a Tocobaga village at the far end of Tampa Bay. The springs had been used since the Stone Age, and even today, are represented as having special healing powers. Though Juan Ponce would certainly have had his ships reconnoitering his vast island, he was in no hurry to set up a colony there. He was rich, forty-seven years old, and quite comfortable at his vast estate in Puerto Rico. He would leave the ongoing reconnaissance to younger men.

Ponce de León establishes the First European Settlement

In mid or late 1520 Juan Ponce learned that a mapping expedition under the command of Francisco de Garay, the governor of Jamaica, had found that *La Florida* was not an island, but part of a landmass that extended to New Spain (Mexico) where Hernán Cortés had found huge treasures. Garay was requesting that the king make him the adelantado of a new province, to be called *Amichel*, extending from the west coast of Mexico, eastward towards Florida.

Ponce de León hastily formed a small expedition to set up a colony in *La Florida* to protect his interests on the new-found mainland. He sent a letter to the king, telling him he was leaving immediately to set up a colony, with two ships and "all the people I can carry." Finally, seven years after first being appointed as the governor of *La Florida*, he sailed to today's Tampa Bay to establish a colony in February 1521. It was the first European colony established in what is now the United States.

After only four months, conflicts with the natives began, resulting in a final battle with the Tocobaga Indians in early July. It resulted in Juan Ponce de León's own mortal wound and the withdrawal of the colonists from Florida. One ship went to Mexico, and Cortés noted its arrival in a letter to the king, saying that Ponce de León had been "defeated" in *La Florida*. The other ship brought Ponce de León to Cuba where he died in July 1521. His many exploits since his arrival in the New World had made him the best-known conquistador and governor in the Indies. His passing was mourned throughout the Indies and in Spain. The Casa de Contratación bestowed a rare honor by naming the bay in which Ponce de León had established a colony as "The Bay of Juan Ponce" on their official world maps.

Other Attempted Settlements Had Failed

The king had appointed Francisco de Garay, the discoverer of the land connection between Florida and Mexico, to govern a new province that Garay had named "Amichel." It included lands extending eastward in the direction of *La Florida* from the River of Palms on the northern coast of Mexico. His attempt to establish a settlement ended almost as soon as it started when he died shortly after he arrived in Mexico in 1523.

The king had also authorized yet another settlement expedition, this one in 1526 on the Atlantic Coast. Lucas Vásquez de Ayllón landed with 600 settlers and 100 horses near the Santee River in present-day South Carolina to establish a settlement and explore the area. It was abandoned in the same year when Ayllón and many other settlers died from starvation or disease. The 150 survivors returned to the island of Hispaniola.

Unknown Lands behind the Coast of the Gulf of Mexico

Other than the islands of the Caribbean and the coasts of Mexico and Central America, little was known of the lands along the coast of the Gulf of Mexico that had been claimed by Spain but were not conquered or populated. The king had appointed numerous governors and captains general of various areas in "the Indies" since they had been discovered by Christopher Columbus in 1492. More than 800 ships had sailed from Spain to the New World since Columbus's discovery, yet little was known of the entire landmass from northern Mexico to the tip of Florida. Each island had its own governor, and Hernán Cortés had been appointed as Captain General of New Spain, later to become known as Mexico. Gold had been found on several islands, and Cortés had conquered the Aztecs, a huge and advanced civilization on the mainland. Its capital, Tenochtitlan, was one of the largest cities in the world, several times the size of the largest cities in Spain, and contained large palaces, plazas, zoos, and gardens. Cortés had found massive amounts of gold and silver, not only in the art objects that had been crafted by the Aztecs but also in the mines that they had established. It was a bonanza, but what about the rest of the landmass that stretched behind the Gulf Coast from New Spain to *La Florida*? The belief persisted: There were other great cities in the New World, and gold was waiting to be found. But where? No one knew, and no one was looking.

Pánfilo de Narváez Seizes an Opportunity

In 1525 there was no governor of the lands that had formerly been the provinces of Francisco de Garay and Juan Ponce de León, as they had both died. One man considered himself to be the logical candidate to replace them both. He was Pánfilo de Narváez, a wealthy man with numerous estates in Cuba. He was a seasoned veteran soldier and captain who had first come to the Indies in 1500. He had participated in the conquest of Jamaica from 1500 to 1510, and as a captain in the conquest of Cuba in 1514 in service to his mentor, Diego Velázquez de Cuéllar (Velázquez). Velázquez had sent ships westward from Cuba and they had discovered the Yucatán. Narváez had been sent to Spain by Velázquez in 1515, seeking to convince King Ferdinand to appoint Velázquez as the adelantado of the Yucatán. Unfortunately for Narváez, King Ferdinand died in January 1516, replaced by his grandson, the 16-year-old King Carlos I. Narvaez spent the next three years in Spain, chasing the traveling court of the new king, to advance the case for the appointment of Velázquez.

While Narvaez was in Spain, Velázquez had appointed another of his captains, Hernán Cortés, to lead a small fleet to explore the coast north of the Yucatán. Cortés had "gone rogue" and had invaded what is now Mexico, claiming all the lands that he conquered for the king and for himself. Narváez returned from Spain in 1520, his mission accomplished ... Velázquez was the newly appointed adelantado of the Yucatán. Narváez was immediately appointed by Velázquez as the Captain General and Lieutenant Governor of the Yucatán, commanding a fleet of 14 ships and more than 800 men, and sent to kill or capture the renegade, Cortés. It was a mission that had failed. It had cost Narváez an eye in combat and had resulted in his loss in battle and four years of his imprisonment by Cortés. From 1520 until 1524, both Velázquez and Narvaez's wife, Maria de Valenzuela, fought to obtain Narvaez's release, both with the royal court in Spain and by offering Cortés ransom. Neither were successful.

Narvaez had finally been freed by Cortés in 1524 and returned to Cuba to learn that his large estates had prospered greatly under the care of his wife, undoubtedly with the substantial help of Velázquez. Narváez, while imprisoned, had become an even richer man, and his mentor Velázquez had become known as "the richest man in the Indies."

Shortly after Narvaez's return to Cuba, Velázquez died. Narvaez determined that it was time for him to become an adelantado himself. He sailed to Spain in late 1525 to petition the king that he be appointed as the adelantado of all the lands from the River of Palms to the Cape of Florida. In his petition, Narváez noted that he was the right man for the job, as he had "born arms in the conquest of these regions for 26 years," and that what he was asking for was less than had been granted to others who had done less, and who had fewer assets with which to carry out their missions. He reminded the king of the "grave responsibility [that] rests on the royal conscience if by delay the conversion of those natives to our holy Catholic Faith should be suspended, and the fruit withheld that is due to the royal patrimony and to your subjects." In other words, "We need to convert the natives to Christianity and find more silver and gold."

Narváez Appointed as an Adelantado

In December 1526, Narváez finally achieved what he had spent a year lobbying to accomplish. The King of Spain agreed, appointing him as the governor and captain general of all the lands from the River of Palms to the Cape of Florida. What was behind the coastline, extending approximately 1,500 miles along the Gulf Coast, was a mystery in 1526. They could not have known that the landmass behind the coast was five times larger than Spain and encompassed more than one million square miles, including portions or all of twenty present-day states, about one-fourth of the current landmass of the United States.

Narváez's assignment was to "explore, conquer, populate and discover all that could be found." He was to govern this land, establishing at least two towns, including two military garrisons, each composed of 100 soldiers, along with other settlers. Across the last three paragraphs of Narváez's approved petition was written, "He must populate." The king also appointed Álvar Núñez Cabeza de Vaca, who had never sailed to the Indies before, as Marshall and Treasurer of the expedition. Fifteen years later, Cabeza de Vaca would gain immortality as the author of a book about the expedition, to become known as the *Relación*. His book and a report dictated by Cabeza de Vaca and the other survivors of the expedition to the scribes of the Viceroy of New Spain are the basis of almost all we know about what happened after Narváez left Spain.

Since the justification of all expeditions into the New World was the conversion of the indigenous population to Christianity, five priests joined the expedition. Narváez also signed on two captains, Alonso de Castillo Maldonado and Andrés Dorantes de Carranza, who brought with him his slave and personal manservant, Estevanico. Their names would be remembered in the centuries to come.

Upon his appointment as governor, Narváez became one of many who would purchase ships and hire ships' captains, pilots, and crews. He recruited soldiers, enlisted colonists, and supplied his ships with all the arms, ammunition, and settlement supplies needed for the 4,300-mile voyage to the New World. Narváez would purchase his ships and supplies and hire his men in Seville as he prepared to sail from Sanlúcar de Barrameda, about sixty miles downriver from Seville. His fleet would only be five of the sixty-eight ships that sailed to the Indies in 1527, but it was certainly the most important as it was the fleet of the king's most recently appointed adelantado.

The Casa de Contratación

The greatest resource to Narváez was the *Casa de Contratación* (House of Contracts, or House of Trade), where he and each of his officers obtained their authority and signed their acceptance of the requirements of the crown. The *Casa* had been established to keep careful track of every person and item that traveled either way between Spain and the Indies. It was also tasked with ensuring that all pilots traveling to the Indies were adequately trained in the use of navigational instruments and had the latest maps, latitudes, and sailing directions derived from a world map known as the *Padrón Real* (royal pattern), the "master map" from which, according to royal decree, all other maps must be derived. The Casa also provided to each pilot a "pilot's manual," known as the *Espejo de Navegantes* (literally, "Navigators' Mirror"), containing conversion tables to calculate latitude and adjust it from the position of the sun and stars. It contained sailing directions, latitudes of key ports, and virtually everything else a pilot or captain would need to know to safely navigate to, and anchor at, a desired destination.

It was likely no coincidence that the king decreed in 1526 that new maps must be created using the latest information derived from ships returning from the Indies. During the year that Narváez had negotiated for his appointment as adelantado, the king had ordered that the *Padrón Real* (Map 1) be redrawn, using all the latest information, to be known thereafter as the *Padrón General* (general pattern). (Map 2) The *Padrón Real* and the *Padrón General* were nine feet by three feet in size, covering the entire world. The Casa was working on the new map in December of 1526 when they learned of Narváez's appointment as governor of all the lands from the River of Palms to the Cape of Florida. Their new map replaced the legend over the northern Gulf Coast that had shown the "Land of Garay" (Map 3) on their old map, with a new legend on the new map, "Land that Pánfilo de Narváez now goes to populate" (Map 4).

From their new world map, the *Casa de Contratación* produced a *Padrón Ordinario*, a smaller but much more detailed map that showed only the portion of the world that Narváez planned to travel (Map 5). The map showed the entire coastline of the then-unnamed Gulf of Mexico, including the area of the greatest interest to Narváez, the *Rio de las Palmas* to the tip of *La Florida*. Unfortunately for Narváez, a returning ship had reported to the Casa that a large bay, *Bahia Honda* (deep bay), was located on the west coast of Florida where none really existed. That information had been included in the *Espejo*, the sailor's manual. Although it was not shown on the new *Padrón General*, it may have been drawn on the smaller and more detailed map provided to Narváez and his pilots. The nonexistent bay, *Bahia Honda*, was described in the *Espejo* as follows: "*Bahía Honda, is on the west coast of La Florida at 29 degrees. This bay is large – ten leagues long and five leagues wide at its mouth. It has three islets at its mouth, and within it is clean and a good place to anchor, very safe for all ships.*" The *Espejo* also described another bay, named the *Bahia de Juan Ponce*. It was described nearly identically, but at a different latitude: "*The Bay of Juan Ponce is on the west coast of La Florida at 27 ¼ degrees. This bay has three small islands at its entrance… this bay is large and clean…along the northern edge at its mouth, near land, it has a long chain of islets.*" The bay being described could only be Tampa Bay. It had recently been named in honor of Juan Ponce de León who had briefly established a settlement before abandoning it due to conflict with the natives that resulted in his mortal wound. It is very likely that the bay had been previously known as *Bahia Honda*. The Casa had made a mistake. There was no large and deep bay north of the Bay of Juan Ponce. What they thought were two different bays was really only one. Those geographic details, ultimately deciding the fate of the expedition, were of little interest at the time. Narváez planned to begin his exploration and conquest at the River of Palms, 1,200 miles away from the bays of *La Florida*.

The Narváez Fleet Sails from Spain

By early June 1527, Narváez had purchased five ships with their captains and crews; employed 600 soldiers and settlers; loaded all the provisions, weapons, and supplies needed for safe passage; provided for a strong landing force; and packed away the provisions, tools, and seeds needed for settlements. He'd acquire his horses, cattle, and pigs in the Indies before leaving for his final destination, the River of Palms. He departed from Spain on June 17, 1527. His first stop would be in the Canary Islands, 800 miles away, to replenish water and firewood. His destination from the Canaries was another 3,500 miles, taking about a month under sail. The trade winds would take him, on the "Road to the Indies," to the island of Hispaniola where he would procure horses, cattle, pigs, and another ship and men, before proceeding to his ultimate destination on the northeast shore of Mexico.

Narváez's expedition did not go as planned. On his arrival in Hispaniola in July or August, 140 of his men disappeared into the wilderness. He had known of this possibility, but it was nevertheless an unwelcome event. Men frequently signed on as soldiers or settlers to gain free passage to the Indies only to desert on arrival to seek their fortunes on their own. Narváez purchased another ship and likely also some horses, cattle, and pigs, and participated in the normal formalities by "logging in" with the Crown's authorities in Santo Domingo. He then took his fleet to Cuba … his home island, where he could regroup. He landed in Santiago, the closest port to his primary estate in San Salvador de Bayamo, about seventy miles inland to the northwest. He knew that in Santiago, and from his own estates, he could obtain many of the men, cattle, pigs, horses, and other provisions that he needed. While in Santiago, Narváez met with an acquaintance who told him that he had supplies that he could provide that were in Trinidad, a port on the southern coast of Cuba, about 300 miles away.

Disaster in Cuba

After provisioning in Santiago, Narváez sailed with his fleet of six ships, bound for his next port, Cabo de Santa Cruz, where he would anchor his fleet and obtain more men and supplies. He sent Cabeza de Vaca on ahead to Trinidad with two ships to pick up more supplies. While Cabeza de Vaca was in Trinidad, a hurricane hit, sinking his two ships and losing sixty men and twenty horses. Hearing of the disastrous news, Narváez sailed to Trinidad, picked up Cabeza de Vaca and the few survivors, and sailed on to Jagua (modern-day Cienfuegos), a well-protected port, where he anchored his four remaining ships for the winter and set out to purchase replacement ships, men, livestock, horses, and supplies.

Months later, in February 1528, Narváez returned to Jagua to rejoin his fleet. He was aboard a brigantine that he had purchased, accompanied by a chief pilot that he had hired to navigate the fleet to the River of Palms. Each ship had a pilot of its own, but the chief pilot, Miruelo, would control the navigation of the flagship and thus the others in the fleet. Narváez had also purchased another ship with a captain named Álvaro de la Cerda. The captain, his crew, forty foot-soldiers, and twelve horsemen were provisioning in Havana, waiting to be joined by the rest of the fleet.

The Narváez Fleet Sets Sail from Jagua

Finally, in February 1528, Narváez had reconstituted a fleet that approximated the one he had left Spain with eight months earlier. With him in Jagua he had a brigantine, which was a smaller "scout" ship used to take soundings for the larger ships when approaching land, and four large ships, plus another ship waiting in Havana. His Jagua complement of 410 sailors, soldiers and settlers included ten married couples. He loaded eighty horses and an unknown number of cattle and pigs then set sail for Havana to join with de la Cerda's ship. Once joined with de la Cerda, the Narváez fleet would consist of his brigantine and five large ships with a combined complement of about 150 ship's crew, ninety-two horsemen and 350 other soldiers and settlers. They would then finally set sail for the River of Palms.

Things, once again, immediately went wrong for Narváez. The fleet, after leaving Jagua on the way to Havana, ran aground and was stranded for two weeks on the famously shallow Canarreo shoals. After getting his brigantine and four large ships afloat again, they headed for an anchorage at the tiny port of Guanaguanico to effect repairs. A major storm hit, damaging one of the larger ships beyond repair. They spent about a month offloading the horses and supplies from the damaged ship and repairing his other ships. The horses from the unseaworthy ship could not be loaded on the other ships, reducing Narváez's horsemen from eighty to sixty. He set sail again, this time with his brigantine and his remaining three large ships, planning to join de la Cerda's ship in Havana, seeking to buy more supplies and perhaps another ship. After rounding the point of Cuba and nearing Havana, strong winds from the south prevented him from reaching port. He had no choice but to let the winds take him north to *La Florida* (Map 6).

Arrival in La Florida

Narváez and his inadequate fleet first saw land in *La Florida* on April 12, 1528, two months after their journey had begun in Jagua. It was most likely the westernmost headland of Florida which extends seven miles west of the entrance to the Bay of Juan Ponce, about twenty miles to the south (Map 7). The fleet, after spotting the headland, headed south along the coast looking for the entrance to the Bay of Juan Ponce. The coastline of Florida is monotonous with no landmarks of any kind. It is fronted by a continuous row of barrier islands, and is extremely shallow, requiring ships to stay well offshore. Since the telescope was not to be invented until 1608, it was difficult for the mariners sailing offshore to see a possible opening to a large bay using eyesight alone. Narváez found a bay and sent his brigantine in to take soundings. They returned to say they had found a large bay that had native dwellings along its inland coastline. Narváez anchored his fleet on April 14, 1528, in water as close to the mouth of the bay as he felt was safe to keep his ships from running aground. It was today's Boca Ciega Bay.

On Good Friday, April 15, 1528, Narváez went ashore with as many men as his ships' service boats could carry, discovering that the large Indian village he had seen had been totally abandoned. They found a small gold rattle, and a building large enough to hold 300 people. Narváez and his men returned to the ship, and on the following day went ashore once again to formally claim the land for Spain and its king, and ordered all aboard the ships to land. He used the brigantine and small service boats to shuttle his people ashore. He had left his last port, Guanaguanico, with sixty horses but eighteen had died along the way. He had his remaining forty-two horses lifted from the holds on slings, put in the water, and allowed to swim ashore. The following day, while the 410 men and women established a camp and unloaded provisions from the ship, a small contingent of Indians arrived. There was no interpreter, but it was obvious from the "signs and menacing gestures" that Narváez was not welcome there. During the holy days of Good Friday, Holy Saturday, and Easter Sunday, Narváez's five priests surely celebrated the appropriate Masses, but no mention of this appears in Cabeza de Vaca's official account except that the bay they had landed in was named the "Bay of the Cross," undoubtedly because the priests had constructed a cross to use during their services.

Narváez Finds the Remnants of the Ponce de León Settlement

The next day, the Spaniards explored inland, reaching a large bay "that seemed to us to go far inland" (present-day Old Tampa Bay). They returned the next day and captured some Indians who led them north along the bays' coastline to the tribe's main village, Tocobaga (today's Safety Harbor) (Map 7). In the village there the Spaniards found "many merchandise boxes from Castile," each containing the body of a dead man covered by a painted deerskin. They also found pieces of linen, cloth, shoes, canvas, and iron. They asked the Indians, by sign language, where the cargo boxes had come from and were told they had found them in a ship that had wrecked nearby. They showed the Indian captives some corn and a small piece of gold. The Indian pointed to the north and indicated that both were very plentiful in a place called "Apalachen," far, far away. With agreement from a priest, Narváez burned the cargo boxes, and the human remains that they contained as "a kind of idolatry." The cargo boxes and other European artifacts were likely those of the Ponce de León settlement seven years earlier, and the bodies those of Indians for whom the boxes had become convenient coffins, keeping the animals from the dead. The priests would not have permitted the burning of the bodies had they thought the dead were Christians, as cremation of Christians was outlawed by the Catholic church. Burning of bodies, even when alive, was permitted only for those who were going to Hell.

Upon returning to his encampment on the bay, Narváez ordered his chief pilot to take the brigantine south to look for the entrance to the Bay of Juan Ponce. If Miruelo failed to find it, he was to continue south to Havana, join up with de la Cerda's ship, and return with more men, horses, and supplies. Although his chief pilot had left, Narváez had at least three other pilots with him who served on his other ships. Each pilot had their instruments, maps, and sailor's manual when they came ashore at Boca Ciega Bay. They were on steady ground and had ample time to make their solar and star sightings and to agree on their latitude, which they undoubtedly determined to be at or about 28° degrees north. The pilots also knew that the Tropic of Cancer, a key latitude used in piloting and navigation, was at 23.4°N, which was by happenstance the latitude of Panuco on the opposite side of the Gulf of Mexico. No one knew better than Narváez and his pilots that if they were separated from their ships, the closest place that they could find other Spaniards was in Panuco, about 800 miles across the Gulf, or more than 1,500 miles around its perimeter. Although New Spain was largely controlled by Narváez's archenemy, Hernán Cortés, Panuco had been made an independent province in 1525, governed by a newly appointed adelantado, Nuño Beltrán de Guzmán (Map 4).

The Inland Exploration Begins

After nearly two weeks had gone by and Miruelo had not returned, Narváez made the fateful decision that would cost him his life, as well as the lives of almost all his men. He determined that it was time to move. There was no hope of establishing a successful settlement where he had landed. There was no food available, and the natives were hostile. He certainly had a strong interest in getting to Apalachen, where the Indians had told him there was plentiful gold, but he had more immediate problems at hand. His ships were anchored outside of the bay, totally unprotected from strong winds or storms that could drive them aground or out to sea. He had no way to get his forty-two horses back aboard the ships. While horses will instinctively swim toward land when lowered into the water on slings, they will not swim out to sea. Even if the horses could somehow be coerced to do so, there was no way to get them back aboard the ships. He also had 410 people to feed, and his supplies were running out. He had left Jagua with plans to be in Havana within a week but had spent two months before he finally reached his present, and very unsafe, anchorage. He would have no choice but to split his land party from his ships and move to a better anchorage and settlement site.

The pilots from the three large ships of his fleet urged Narváez to travel north, to a huge bay that was about a day's sail away. It would give the ships a safe anchorage and perhaps provide better sources of food. They knew they were at about 28°N. Their sailing directions said that *Bahia Honda* was at 29°N and that it was a deep and protected anchorage for their ships. One degree of latitude was only about sixty-eight miles. The pilots told Narváez that the huge bay extended thirty miles inland. If the men on land went north along the coast and the ships also sailed north, they could rejoin there, as the huge bay to the north would be "impossible to miss." Miruelo, on his return, could easily find their ships at anchorage there.

Narváez held a meeting of his officers as required by the king when his appointment as adelantado was approved. It required him to reach an agreement with his key officers before making any major decisions... and this was a major one. All knew that their ships were a lifeline home. Should they lose their connection with their ships, they'd be stranded in this godforsaken place. Cabeza de Vaca wrote that he had opposed the idea of separating the ships from the land expedition but had been out-voted by the other officers, a claim that he probably made in his *Relación* to convince the king that the disastrous result would not have occurred had he been in charge. After considerable discussion among the officers, it was decided that they must go north to seek the large bay.

Narváez was acutely aware, due to his earlier encounters in which he had captured Indians and burned the Indian dead in the sacred To-cobaga burial ground, that the local Indians were hostile. They would undoubtedly attack when and where they had the opportunity. He would need a large and well-armed force to travel along an unknown coastline.

The ships, with their crews and the ten women, would sail north along the coast while Narváez would follow the coastline north with his horses and men, meeting at the huge bay that lay nearby and was "impossible to miss." Narváez was unaware that the harbor that he had sought, the deep bay extending thirty miles inland, was to his south. Miruelo had missed it as he sailed south because the entrance to the bay was guarded by a single large island and smaller islands and sandbars, making the entrance nearly impossible to see when sailing in safely deep water off-shore. Narváez was unaware that he had already discovered a portion of it, now known as Old Tampa Bay, on his first inland exploration across today's Pinellas peninsula from his landing place on Boca Ciega Bay (Map 7). Unfortunately for Narváez and his land expedition, there was no large bay to the north.

Narváez assembled his men and forty remaining horses for the inland trek to the north. They had already eaten two of their horses and had little left to provide food for 410 people. The provisions provided to each of the 300 men of the land expedition were meager, consisting of a pound of hardtack and a half pound of salt pork. They'd have to live off the land, finding food, fresh water, and grazing for their horses along the way.

As the land expedition traveled north, it became harder and harder to see the coastline. In crossing a river that they encountered, Narváez lost his first man when he and his horse drowned. The starving expeditionaries buried their comrade and ate his horse. After about ten days of travel during which they had encountered no large bay extending thirty miles inland, they reached a river that was very difficult to cross. Cabeza de Vaca and the other officers urged Narváez to send a party to follow the river to see if it emptied into a large bay, where their ships might be found. An expedition was sent to the river mouth where it emptied into the Gulf, but the water in the area was far too shallow for ships, and it did not "extend thirty miles inland" as the *Espejo* said. Narváez determined to keep traveling north. Little was to be gained if they tried to return to their original landing site.

An Expedition of Conquest Becomes One of Survival

The Narváez exploration to the north involved near starvation and frequent conflict with the Indians. For fifteen days, all they could find to eat were hearts of palm. Eight of his men were killed by Indians along the way. Many others were wounded, and all were starving and exhausted from carrying their armor and weapons across rivers and through tangled terrain. After traveling by land for approximately 250 miles, the surviving members of the expedition reached the St. Marks River, south of present-day Tallahassee, in July 1528. They had never encountered their ships or a large bay extending thirty miles inland, and they had not reached the huge amounts of gold in Apalachen and never would. Their expedition of conquest and discovery had changed to one of survival.

Narváez knew that he had two choices: He could continue to walk along the perimeter of the Gulf to Panuco, crossing rivers, which could be nearly impossible due to their current or width, making his men vulnerable to attack; or he could build boats, using them to hug the coast to sail around the perimeter. That choice would avoid constant attacks by the Indians with the additional advantage that if ships came searching for him, he would be easier to find.

The second option was his only real choice. In his current encampment, he was losing men nearly daily to Indians, starvation, and illness.

Many of his men were sick or wounded. He knew that he had no chance of surviving constant Indian attacks. Indians had just killed ten of his men in a single day when he had dispatched them to go fishing to get food for the others. Sailing close to shore would allow him to stop for food and water along the way. He had no other choice than to build rafts or small boats to sail the coastal route. Fortunately, he had at least two carpenters and an ample supply of wood nearby. He could make bellows from horsehides to create fires hot enough to melt their iron weapons to create tools. He had plenty of swords and knives to convert to saws, and shirts from which to make sails. He had a carpenter who could "make pipes from wood." They could make rope from horsehair manes and tails, and, luckily, an abundant supply of the saw palmetto, a plant from which it was easy to harvest fibers to use in lieu of oakum for caulking the boats, sealing it with pitch from the local pines. Narváez knew that his men could capture or steal Indian canoes to serve as outriggers for his heavily laden boats. He had many men who could work all daylight hours every day. Narváez ordered the construction of boats to begin. His ships' carpenters came up with a plan. It would take five boats approximately thirty-five feet long. Each boat would have sails made up of shirts. The sails would be used when winds were favorable, and they'd use oars when it was not. The boats would be slow and hard to maneuver, but with luck, and if strongly built, they would stay afloat. It would take months to build the boats. They had no food, so they would raid local Indian villages for corn. The corn, their own horses, and an occasional fish, would become their food. They'd kill one horse every three days. The horses were by now very thin. The meat from each horse would provide meager rations when spread over three days and divided among 282 men. Only the fit would survive. During the ensuing months, Narváez lost forty more men to illness, combat, or starvation, leaving him with only 242 survivors when his boats were finally completed.

Leaving the Bay of Horses

In September 1528, the survivors boarded their five newly constructed boats and set forth from the place where they had eaten their horses and buried fifty of their comrades. They named it "The Bay of Horses." They set sail along the shores of the Gulf of Mexico in the direction of Panuco, more than 1,000 miles away. As their small fleet headed west, they made landfalls in present-day Alabama, Mississippi, and Louisiana seeking food and water to continue their journey. They met with numerous native tribes, likely becoming the first White and Black men to be encountered by most of those Native American tribes. Some were helpful, providing food and water. Others weren't. Narváez lost many of his men as they traveled along the coast. Five died when they drank salt water because no fresh water was to be found. Others were killed or captured by Indians as the small fleet stopped along the way. Among them was Doroteo Teodoro, likely the first Greek to try to settle in America. Doroteo was the man who had taught them to use pine tree pitch in lieu of tar to seal their boats. He and his slave were captured by Indians and never seen again.

In December 1528, about three months after leaving the Bay of Horses, the five boats had miraculously sailed 800 miles westward to a point somewhere seaward of present-day Galveston Island. It was then that a severe storm struck, separating the boats, and sweeping an estimated eighty-two men ashore. About 150 men were lost at sea. The survivors were widely scattered in small groups along the forty-five-mile coastline of the barrier islands guarding today's Galveston Bay. Many of the survivors died of starvation or illness or were killed by local natives. Pánfilo de Narváez drowned when his crudely repaired boat was swamped by the sea. It was an ignominious ending for the proud conquistador who had participated in the conquests of Jamaica and Cuba, commanded an army of 800 men in Mexico, and was the governor of the largest territory ever assigned by the king.

The Survivors Are Enslaved for Six Years, then Escape

One of the isolated groups that had washed ashore resorted to cannibalism until the last one died. The other survivors became slaves of the natives in the Galveston Island area. During the period of his enslavement, Cabeza de Vaca was allowed to become a trader, traveling among the local tribes, and had become a "medicine man" using the power of prayer and home remedies to "cure" the natives, a skill he taught to his companions.

In 1534, six years after their captivity, only four of the expedition survived. The four men, Álvar Núñez Cabeza de Vaca, Alonso de Castillo Maldonado, Andrés Dorantes de Carranza, and Estevanico, the African slave of Dorantes, finally escaped from the tribe that had enslaved them, heading inland away from the coast. The Spaniards and the African slave were the first men of Europe and Africa to enter the American West. During the first weeks, perhaps months, of their wandering, the four were literally naked and unarmed, scrounging for whatever food and water they were able to find.

As the foursome moved further west, they began to encounter native Indian tribes, the first encounters between many tribes of Native

Americans and the White and Black men. Estevanico became the group's interpreter, learning sign and native languages. He was the person sent in advance, as he was the most able to communicate with the natives. Cabeza de Vaca and the others were looked upon in awe, as men of their races had never been seen before. All four were accepted as medicine men as they used religious rituals and minor surgery to heal.

The survival journey took them across present-day Texas, Mexico, and perhaps as far north as New Mexico. All four posed, and were treated as, powerful medicine men by the Native Americans as they used prayer, rituals, minor surgery, and home remedies in their "healing" of the natives. The wanderers were treated as near-gods as they traveled west, always accompanied by hundreds of native admirers who bestowed their most prized possessions as gifts to the four, including meat, buffalo hides, ornaments, and sacred gourd rattles. Each tribe would escort them to the lands of another as they moved slowly inland. During their survival journey, the four travelers had been the first Europeans, and the first African, to see the American Bison. Cabeza de Vaca wrote, "These animals come from the north all the way to the coast of Florida where they scatter, crossing the land for more than 400 leagues. All along their range, through the valleys where they roam, people who live near there descend to live off them and take inland a great quantity of their hides."

The Four Survivors Reach the Shores of the Pacific and Salvation

In April 1536, the four wanderers finally reached salvation. As they approached the shores of the Pacific Ocean, they encountered Spanish "slavers" near San Miguel in the new Spanish province of Nueva Galicia. The incredulous slavers learned that the three Spaniards and the African slave had survived the Narváez expedition that had disappeared in *La Florida* in 1528. The survivors had traveled more than 2,000 miles over eight years, completing a survival journey that would be written about and studied for the next 500 years.

Cabeza de Vaca and the others learned that the newly appointed Viceroy of New Spain, and the main Spanish settlement, were in Mexico City, 1,000 miles to the south. The four survivors had been told of an advanced civilization of seven great cities to the north in an area called "Cibola." The local Indians had told them of being employed as migrant workers by the people of Cibola, who wore fine clothes of cotton, had much turquoise, and lived in large cities with buildings of many stories. But the survivors did not attempt to find Cibola; they turned south to Mexico City.

Upon arrival in Mexico City on July 25, 1536, the explorers had traveled more than 3,000 miles over eight years and three months. The four survivors dictated their report to the scribes of Antonio de Mendoza, the Viceroy of New Spain, and added that they had heard of, but not seen, great cities of Cibola to the north. Their tales of their discoveries would inform the two largest expeditions ever to explore the American South and Southwest.

In 1537 Cabeza de Vaca returned to Spain, hoping to be appointed as the new governor of *La Florida*. Unfortunately for Cabeza de Vaca, Hernando de Soto had recently returned, as a very wealthy man, from his participation with Pizarro in the conquest of Peru. King Carlos had just appointed Soto as the new governor of *La Florida*, replacing the missing Narváez. Cabeza de Vaca told his adventures to the king and Soto and wrote of his survival journey in his *Relación* that he presented to the king.

(It was published as a book in 1542, becoming the first book to describe the geography, flora, fauna, wildlife, and peoples of North America.) He told Soto and the king of the large amounts of gold that the Indians had said were in a place in north Florida, called Apalachen, that he had been unable to reach. He was urged to join Soto in his expedition to *La Florida* to find the gold of Apalachen, but declined to do so. Cabeza de Vaca believed that he had earned a position as an adelantado, and the king agreed, appointing him as the Governor of the Río de Plata region in South America.

The next expedition to La Florida would be commanded by a third adelantado who would attempt the mission that had killed Ponce de León and Pánfilo de Narváez ... the conquest of *La Florida*. It would kill Hernando de Soto, too.

The Hernando de Soto Expedition

Hernando de Soto financed a large expedition to return to the place that Cabeza de Vaca had spoken of, planning to land at the bay that Cabeza de Vaca had described but had never seen himself. Cabeza de Vaca had described the large bay in his *Relación*: "This port is the best in the world, and it enters inland seven or eight leagues. And it is six fathoms deep [thirty feet] at the entrance and five near land." This information was reported to him after he returned to Spain and met with those who had searched for Narváez for an entire year. Miruelo, his pilot, had returned from Cuba accompanied by de la Cerda's ship as he had been instructed, only to learn that Narváez was no longer there. In his search, Miruelo had found that the entrance to the large bay that extended thirty miles inland was only fifteen miles south of their original landing site and that it led to the village on its distant shore where Narváez had found "many boxes from Castile" (Map 7).

On February 30, 1539 (Julian calendar), Hernando de Soto landed in Tampa Bay with the largest expedition ever to explore North America. It consisted of 500 men, 237 horses, 500 head of livestock, and 300 pigs. Upon landing, Soto encountered Juan Ortiz, a survivor of the search for the missing Narváez expedition eleven years earlier. According to an account of the Soto expedition written by a chronicler of the time, Gonzalo Fernández Oviedo y Valdés, Juan Ortiz had been captured by the chief of the tribe, who had decided to kill Ortiz, but his life had been saved when the chief's daughter had begged that his life be spared. Ortiz later escaped and lived as a native with the neighboring tribe. Juan Ortiz became Soto's interpreter and guide and led them as they retraced the path of Narváez's expedition northward toward Apalachen. Failing to find gold, they continued their exploration to what are now today's states of Georgia, South Carolina, North Carolina, Tennessee, Alabama, Mississippi, Arkansas, Oklahoma, and Texas. Juan Ortiz died during the winter of 1541/42 and Soto died near the Mississippi River, probably near present-day Ferriday, Louisiana on May 21, 1542. The 311 survivors built boats on the banks of the Mississippi River and sailed downstream and into the Gulf of Mexico. They arrived in Panuco, Mexico in September 1543. They had traveled more than 4,000 miles over four years and seven months. Nearly one-half of the men of the expedition had perished, including its leader, Hernando de Soto, who had become the third adelantado to die in the quest to conquer *La Florida*. The expedition had failed to find any of the riches that they had sought.

The Fray Marcos de Niza Expedition

Simultaneously with the start of the Hernando de Soto expedition, another expedition was being undertaken…this one based on the stories told by Cabeza de Vaca, Dorantes, Maldonado, and Estevanico of the great cities to the north. Sometime after Estevanico had arrived in Mexico City in 1536, he had apparently been freed. He was known thereafter as Estevan de Dorantes. In 1539, the Viceroy of New Spain determined that it was time to find the cities of Cibola that were somewhere far beyond his northernmost outpost, where Estevanico and his three companions had ended their survival journey. He decided that an exploration should begin in Sinaloa, 1,000 miles north of Mexico City, and travel north from there into unknown and unexplored territory. The mission would be one of peace and there would be no soldiers or arms. He instructed Fray Marcos de Niza, an Italian Franciscan Friar, to form a small expedition north to find the cities. He told Fray Marcos to spread the word that he had outlawed the enslavement of any native Indians. He retained Estevan to lead, as the advance scout, the mission to the north in March 1539, instructing Estevan to obey Fray Marcos as he would obey the Viceroy himself. The expedition included only Estevan, two Friars, and an unknown number of natives as guides. Its purpose was to assure the Indian tribes that slavery had been outlawed and to seek the great cities in Cibola. In travels north, through present-day Mexico, Estevan was treated as a medicine man with great healing powers, as he was known from his previous survival journey. Natives ran in advance to tell other tribes of his coming, and that no longer would the Spanish be capturing and enslaving Indians. It was now safe for them to return to live in their villages. Estevan received massive tributes from each village and tribe. After crossing his trail from his earlier survival journey, he headed northeast into unknown territory, always traveling far ahead of Fray Marcos de Niza. Two Greyhounds, never seen before by the natives, always accompanied him. Fray Marcos and Estevan had worked out a messaging system. If Estevan was getting closer to Cibola, he sent runners back to Fray Marcos with a wooden cross. The more promising the goal appeared, the larger the cross that Estevan would send back to Fray Marcos. The crosses sent back by Estevan grew larger and larger as the journey progressed.

Estevan traveled ahead of de Niza and entered what is today's Arizona and, with a small retinue of northern Mexican Indians, east into what today is New Mexico. Estevan had become the first non-Native American to discover these lands. In entering the area known as Cibola, 700 miles northeast of Sinaloa, he first encountered the A:shiwi (later named the *Zuñi* by the Spanish) in a city named Hawikku.

The A:shiwi were unlike any Indian tribe that Estevan had encountered before. They represented a totally new and alien culture to those that he had experienced in his prior travels. Hawikku consisted of huge buildings, 3-4 stories tall, covering an acre or more with hundreds of rooms. They were built of clay bricks containing mica that sometimes glinted in the sun...like gold. The A:shiwi spoke a "language isolate" not spoken by other tribes in the area, and practiced their own unique and secretive religion, totally different from the tribes far to the south. They wore clothing woven of cotton, like the frocks worn by Franciscan Friars. They had occupied the same area for more than 1,000 years. The area of Cibola included other villages that were the home of the A:shiwi as well as of several other tribes. They were later named "pueblos" by the Spanish.

The Death of Estevan

Estevan arrived in Hawikku in July 1539. His coming was known, as native runners preceded him. There are two versions of what happened to Estevan when he reached Hawikku. Fray Marcos de Niza reported when he returned to Mexico City, that his Indian guides fleeing from Hawikku had told him that they had been attacked by the A:shiwi, and that Estevan had been killed. There is no supporting evidence that this is true, nor is there any evidence that de Niza had actually seen the city of Hawikku as he reported that he had. He was always many days behind Estevan, and it's unlikely that he ever got close enough to see Hawikku. What happened to Estevan, according to A:shiwi (now known as Zuni) oral history, is that he represented himself as a medicine man flourishing a gourd rattle adorned with owl feathers. Gourds were very sacred to the A:shiwi, used only inside kivas by tribal medicine men, and owl feathers were a symbol of death. Estevan was captured and held by the A:shiwi. The A:shiwi religion consisted of many secret societies led by elders, and a chief (cacique) who met to discuss what to do with Estevan. The ruling was made that Estevan was falsely representing himself as a medicine man, as he had displayed the sacred gourd outside of the kiva, bore owl feathers, and his powerful gestures with outspread arms were unlike those of a real medicine man. The A:shiwi penalty for anyone, whether A:shiwi or not, pretending to be a medicine man, was death. The A:shiwi executed Estevan in Hawikku.

Whether or not Marcos de Niza's or the A:shiwi account is the right one, Estevan de Dorantes died in Hawikku in 1539. He was about thirty-nine years old. He had traveled from Morocco to Spain, to the islands in the Indies, to *La Florida*, to unexplored territories along the Gulf Coast, to the American West, to Mexico, and then to his destiny in a land that did not yet have a name. He had traveled more than 10,000 miles, ever loyal to his master, Dorantes, and to his Viceroy after he was freed. Centuries later, books would be devoted to Estevanico and to the story of his extraordinary life.

The Francisco Vásquez de Coronado Expedition

Fray Marcos de Niza had never reached Hawikku and was encamped nearby. When Indian runners came to tell him that Estevan had been killed, he returned to Mexico City. He reported the death of Estevan and the existence of a huge city he had seen in Cibola. To seek the "cities of gold" and perhaps to avenge the death of Estevan, an enormous expedition, led by Francisco Vásquez de Coronado and guided by Fray Marcos, traveled north to conquer Hawikku. The expedition of February 1540 consisted of 240 mounted soldiers, 60 infantry, an estimated 800 Indians, and countless cattle, mules, and sheep. They reached Hawikku and discovered that de Niza had misled Coronado about the riches of the city. Upon discovery that there was no "city of gold" at Hawikku, Marcos de Niza was sent back to Mexico City in disgrace.

Coronado conquered Hawikku and pressed on, looking for the cities of gold. He explored today's Arizona, New Mexico, Texas, Oklahoma, and Kansas. His expedition included the first Europeans to see the Grand Canyon. Neither De Soto nor Coronado knew of the other's expedition occurring nearly simultaneously. The Hernando de Soto expedition was exploring west from its original landing in the Bay of Juan Ponce, while Coronado's was heading east. It is very likely that when they reached today's Texas, they were, unknowingly, a few hundred miles from each other. The Coronado expedition, after reaching Kansas, turned back and returned to Mexico in April 1542. They had traveled more than 3,500 miles in a period of two years and four months, looking for cities of gold that were not there.

The Legacies of the Narváez Expedition

The greatest legacy of the Narváez expedition is Álvar Núñez Cabeza de Vaca's *Relación*. It not only recounted the travails of the entire expedition, providing the names of key participants and the extent of the extraordinary journey of the four survivors, but it also became the first book ever published about the geography, peoples, wildlife, flora, and fauna of inland North America. An additional legacy is that the Narváez survivors motivated and informed three following expeditions, two of which are the largest and longest ever to explore North America.

Between 1528 and 1543, the Spanish had undertaken four important expeditions of discovery of the American South and Southwest. From the tales told by the survivors of the ill-fated Narváez expedition when they arrived in New Spain in 1536 sprang the Fray Marcos de Niza expedition of 1539, the Hernando de Soto expedition of 1539, and the Francisco Vázquez de Coronado Expedition of 1540. The four expeditions involved more than 1,200 Europeans of which fewer than 600 had survived. Two adelantados, Pánfilo de Narváez and Hernando de Soto, had died on their expeditions, as had the intrepid African slave, Estevanico. The combined expeditions had traveled more than 15,000 miles through unknown territory in their quests for riches that were never found.

The expeditions of Coronado and De Soto introduced horses, cattle, and pigs into what is now the United States for the first time. It has been theorized that escaping, abandoned, or stolen animals were the original sources of some of the herds that later grew to become a part of the millions of horses, cattle, and pigs that flourished in the coming centuries in the South, Midwest, and West. Hundreds of years later the fabled Plains Indians would hunt the buffalo on horseback, and the "cowboy" would seek his fortune rounding up the millions of cattle that roamed free in Florida and in the west.

The expeditions represented the first documented explorations of the North American continent, all occurring more than 250 years before the Lewis & Clark expedition would head west from Missouri.

Today throughout the south and southwest of the United States there are a multitude of Coronado and De Soto highways, monuments, parks, and schools. A forest in Colorado and an automobile once built in Detroit add to the tributes to those who bravely ventured so far from home to explore vast new territories in a New World.

Although all of the evidence demonstrates that Juan Ponce de León established his colony in or near Safety Harbor, and there is no evidence to the contrary, nothing marks the site of the first European colony established in today's United States. Similarly, the Narváez expedition was the first inland exploration of North America and became the most remarkable survival journey in the history of the New World, yet there are no Narváez, Cabeza de Vaca, or Estevanico monuments or parks.

The remarkable expedition that began in St. Petersburg, Florida that produced the first book published about inland North America, included an African slave who "discovered" Arizona and New Mexico, and informed the largest and longest expeditions of discovery ever to explore the United States is marked only by a small sign near a beach and an ancient Indian midden on the shore of Boca Ciega Bay. It is scant remembrance of the brave and venturesome men and women who first came to settle *La Florida* a half-millennium ago.

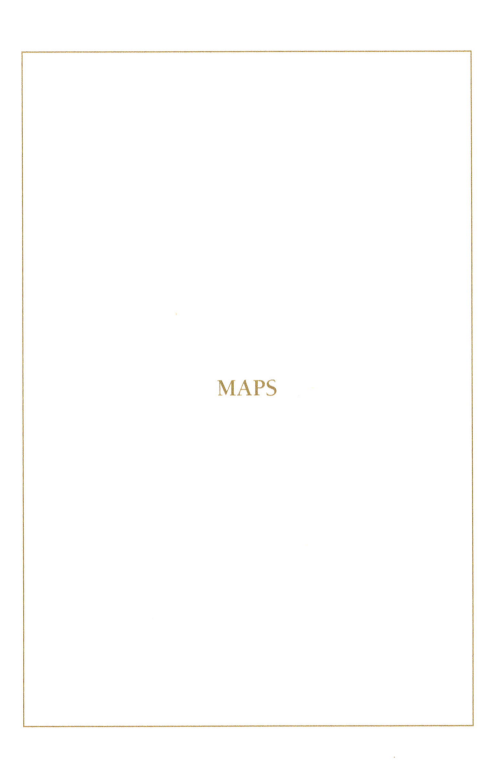

MAPS

The full 1527 and 1529 maps included in this section best demonstrate the difficulty encountered by past historians in attempting to discover locations and landing sites. It is impossible to print a three-foot by two-foot map in a book that would allow toponyms (place names) to be read. For this reason, books rarely show maps that were produced in very large scale, and if they do, the toponyms are unreadable.

Only modern technology allows high-resolution scanning of very large maps, and the enlargement of selected areas, allowing toponyms to be read. When even the enlargement after high-resolution scanning does not provide great clarity, it can be enhanced via artificial intelligence, as has been accomplished with the maps in this book.

The originals of the maps in this book are scanned from maps in *Die Beiden Altesten General-Karten von Amerika*, published by J.G. Kohl in 1860. The book contains two maps, each 27" by 36" that are folded and inserted, and not bound in. They are copies of the North and South American portions of the original world maps dated 1527 and 1529 that Kohl was permitted to duplicate by the Grand Ducal Library in Weimar, Germany.

The 1527 and 1529 original maps still exist at the Herzogin Anna Amalia Bibliothek and have been placed online. Unfortunately, the originals are very faded, and the scan is not high resolution, so does not allow enlargement of all the details, but one can see enough to determine that Kohl's copies were faithful reproductions of the originals.

The 1527 and 1529 maps, copied by J.G. Kohl in 1860, have been digitized and provided by the author to the University of Florida's George A. Smathers Digital Collection, and now are available to the public online.

1. The "1529" Ribero World Map. Copied by J.G. Kohl in 1860.

Title: *"Carta universal en que se contiene todo lo que del mundo se ha descubierto fasta agora. Hizola Diego Ribero cosmographo de su magestad, An[n]o de 1529, e[n] Sevilla"* ("World Map containing all that has been discovered in the world that Diego Ribero, cosmographer of His Majesty, made in Seville in 1529"). This original copy by J.G. Kohl is 27" by 36" and represents only the North and South America portions of the Ribero world map.

Although dated 1529, the geographic details are those of 1526 or earlier, as noted on Map 3. Note that this map and the 1527 world map (Map 2), are examples of the great difficulty faced by those wishing to reproduce a map in a book. Virtually nothing on the map is readable. Until recently, the only way to produce an enlargement of a smaller area was by taking a photo of the map and enlarging it, losing fine details. Scholars of the past have had to accomplish most of their research without the use of detailed maps. This has led some to incorrect conclusions as to landing sites and travels of early expeditions to the New World.

This map has twelve lengthy legends (or colophons) that describe people, places or events. These lengthy legends would not be included on a map intended for use in navigation or as detail necessary in producing another map of a smaller selected area. This provides an immediate clue that this map was decorated after its geographical features were drawn.

King Carlos had decreed in 1526 that the official world map maintained by the *Casa de Contratación*, the *Padrón Real*, was to be replaced by a new and more accurate map, the *Padrón General*.

This map is the obsolete *Padrón Real*. It is dated 1529, the year that it was presented, and not 1526 when its original geographic elements and toponyms had been drawn.

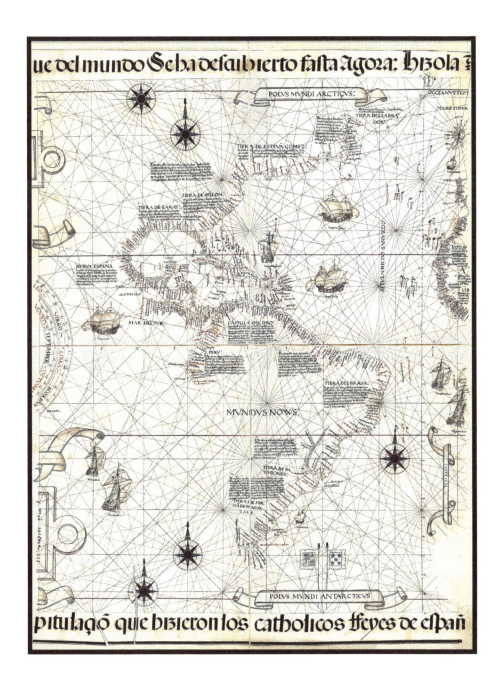

2. The 1527 World Map, attributed to Hernando Colón.
Copied by J.G. Kohl in 1860.

Its full title is: "*Carta Universal en se contiene todo lo que del mundo se ha descubierto fasta aora: Hizola un cosmógrafo de SM Anno MDXXVII*" ("Universal map containing everything that has been discovered so far in the world: It was made by a cosmographer of H.M. [His Majesty] in 1527"). This original copy by J.G. Kohl is 27" by 36" and represents only the North and South America portions of the Colón world map.

Like the problems highlighted in the description of the Ribero map (Map 1), when a map of this size is reduced for publication in a book, all detail is lost.

It is most commonly attributed to Hernando Colón, the son of Cristobal Colón (Christopher Columbus). Colón was in a senior position at the *Casa de Contratación* in Seville when the map was created, and it was to Colón that King Carlos I had issued the directive to create a new world map in 1526.

Note that this map contains no legends (or colophons) that describe people places or events. It was not decorated for presentation, as was the case in the "1529" Ribero map (Map 1).

This map features a latitude scale that is barely discernible when the map is copied and published in a book. One must have the original two-foot by three-foot map to identify the latitude scale and from that determine the latitude for selected places. The latitude scale on this map has the Tropic of Cancer at 23.5°N. It is 23.4°N using today's GPS, a difference of seven miles.

This map is the first *Padrón General,* created on instructions from the king in 1526.

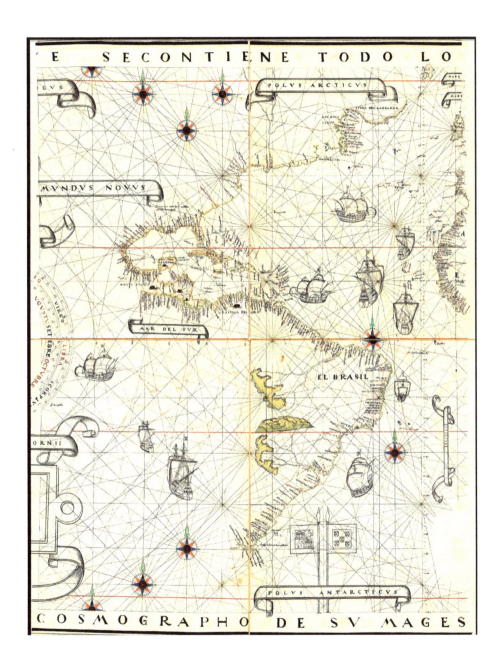

For God, Glory, and Gold

3. "1529" Ribero Map (Detail)

This enlargement of the Gulf of Mexico area establishes the fact that this map shows the world as it was known in 1526, not in 1529. The land area immediately above the north shore of the Gulf of Mexico is titled the "Land of Garay" and to the right is the "Land of Ayllón." The legend below Garay states, "Land of Garay. Along this entire coast and that of the Licentiate Ayllón and the land of Esteban Gómez, it is not anticipated that gold will be discovered as it has been in New Spain because [these lands] are so distant from the Tropic." Under Ayllón, it states: "Land of Ayllón, which he discovered and returned to settle because it is land well-disposed to produce bread [wheat] and wine and all things from Spain: [Ayllón] died here from disease."

Francisco de Garay had been appointed as the Spanish governor of the lands above the northern Gulf Coast in 1519 but had died in 1523 without ever establishing a settlement. A map that was created in 1529 would not state that "it is not anticipated that gold will be found" by Garay, nor that he was the governor of that area since he died in 1523. Similarly, Ayllón had established his settlement in 1526 and died the same year. A 1529 map would not show him as the governor of that territory.

In 1526, Pánfilo de Narváez was appointed as adelanto, replacing Garay, who had died in 1523. A 1529 map would not attribute Narváez's lands to Garay.

When the attribution of the lands to Ayllón and Garay is noted, in connection with legends on the map that include reference to information that was added after 1526, it becomes clear that the geographical elements and toponyms of this "1529" map were drawn in 1526 or earlier, and that some of the legends were added or corrected later. An example is in the legend re Ayllón, described above, which has a forward-looking description of his proposed settlement, and a note added at the end: "died here from disease."

This map was the original *Padrón Real*, made obsolete by the requirement of the king to create a new world map in 1526. It was enhanced for presentation in 1529.

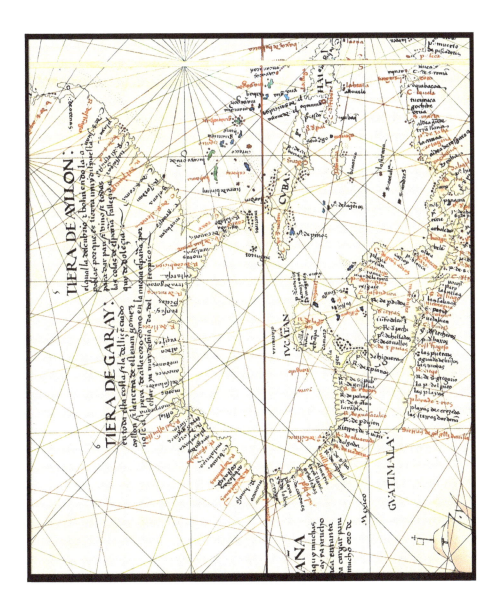

4. 1527 Colón Map. (Detail)

This enlargement of the Gulf of Mexico area eliminates the "Tierra de Garay" and "Tierra de Ayllón" headings that had been included on the "1529" Ribero map (Map 3). They are removed and replaced with, *"Tierra que aora ba a poblar panfilo de narbaez"* ("Lands that Pánfilo de Narváez now goes to populate").

Narváez was appointed adelantado of the area from the *Rio de las Palmas* in Mexico to the Cape of Florida in December 1526, the same year that King Carlos I had ordered that the current world map, the *Padrón Real*, was to be replaced by a new one, the *Padrón General*. This is the new world map, the *Padrón General*.

Panuco, the goal for Narváez in his survival journey, is on the coast of Mexico. The toponym is partially obscured by the bold red Tropic of Cancer line on the map.

Since the map states that Narváez is "now going," it indicates that it was drawn in early-to-mid 1527, as Narváez had left Spain for the Indies in June.

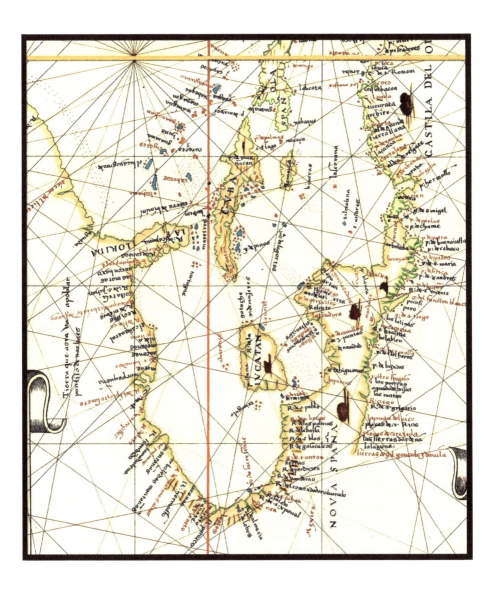

5. 1527 Colón map. (Detail of River of Palms to Cape of Florida.)

This enlargement of the Gulf of Mexico coastal area includes the entire coastline from the River of Palms (*"Las Palmas"*) on the northeastern coast of Mexico, to the Cape of *La Florida*.

This map is not intended to represent a much more detailed map, a *Padrón Ordinario*, that would have been provided to Narváez before he left Spain. That map would have included much more detail. However, since the king had mandated that all maps had to be derived from the *Padrón General*, including place names and latitudes, the information on this map would have been included on Narváez's maps.

Of the forty-four waterways named on the Gulf Coast of Mexico, only one, the *B. de Juhan Ponce*, is identified as a bay. All other waterways are identified as rivers (Río).

Toponyms for *Las Palmas* and *B. de Juhan Ponce*, and arrows, have been added to point to the inscriptions on the map, which are otherwise hard to find. The toponyms on the map are both in red, which was reserved by mapmakers for the most important places.

This map identifies the Bay of Juan Ponce at the latitude of 27.5°N, the exact latitude of the entrance to Tampa Bay.

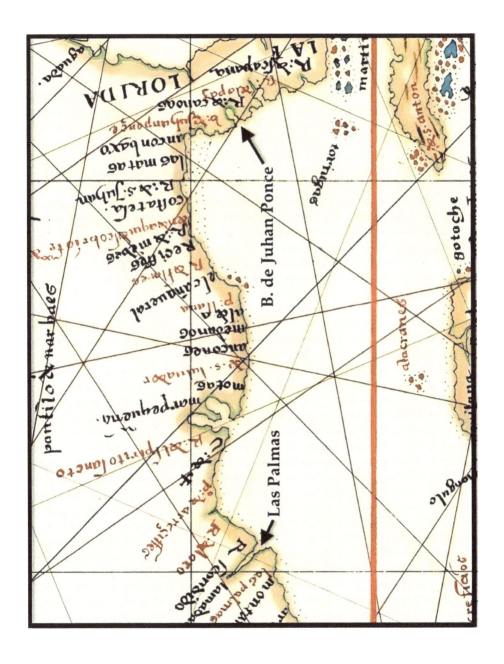

6. 1527 Colón map. (Detail of La Florida.)

This enlargement of the Florida portion of the 1527 Colón world map provides the names of three rivers south of the *B. de Juhan Ponce* (Bay of Juan Ponce). Ascending from south to north, they are *R. Scapana*, *R. de la Paz* (River of Peace), and *R. de Canoas* (River of Canoes).

It is thought that the River of Scapana is derived from a derivation of the Indian name "Estantapaca" or "Escampaba," the name of the main village of the Calusa Indians, located at Estero Bay, well south of today's Charlotte Harbor.

R. de la Paz is located on the map at 26.5°N just south of the entrance to Charlotte Harbor. A river named "Peace River" flows into Charlotte Harbor today. The *R. de Canoas* is located at 27°N, the entrance to today's Myakka River, which also flows into Charlotte Harbor.

The author theorizes that the rivers got their names when Ponce de León first visited the Charlotte Harbor area on his discovery expedition of 1513. He had met with natives at a river to plan to discuss peace with their chief, agreeing to meet at another river. On arrival at the meeting place, Juan Ponce's men were attacked by Indians in eighty canoes. Thus, the names River of Peace and River of Canoes. The Peace River still exists today, flowing into Charlotte Harbor.

This map shows "Tortugas" (today's Dry Tortugas) due south of the Bay of Juan Ponce. The Dry Tortugas are directly south of the entrance to Tampa Bay. It also indicates that the Bay of Juan Ponce is at 27.5°N, the exact GPS latitude of the entrance to Tampa Bay.

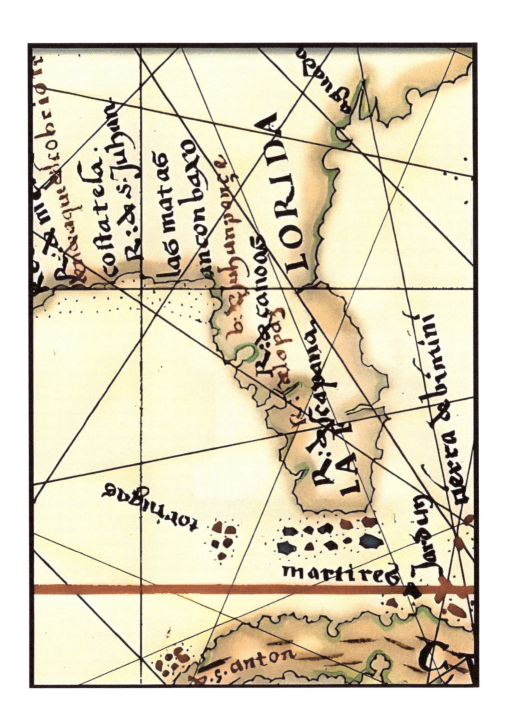

7. The Landing Sites.
The Narváez Expedition Landing Site and the discoveries at Safety Harbor.
That Narváez landed on the shore of Boca Ciega Bay and traveled inland to today's Safety Harbor (Tocobaga) is certain. Both the *Relación* and the "Joint Report" describe the first inland expedition as a one-day walk to the shore of a large bay that appeared to go far inland followed the next day by a walk around the shore of the bay to an Indian village "at the back of the bay" where they found "many boxes from Castile." In the final chapter of the *Relación*, Cabeza de Vaca wrote that the pilot, Miruelo, who had returned from Havana and had gone looking for Narváez, had found, only fifteen miles south of their original landing site, the opening to the huge bay that extended thirty miles inland and that "it was the same one that we had discovered, where we found the crates from Castile." The fact that the place that they found the cargo boxes from Castile was reachable overland from the original landing site as well as by entering and traversing Tampa Bay, clearly establishes both the landing site and the site where they found the cargo boxes.

The Juan Ponce de León Settlement Site at or near Safety Harbor.
Strong evidence exists that Ponce de León established the first European colony in today's United States in Tampa Bay, and specifically in "Old Tampa Bay" near Safety Harbor (Tocobaga).
- "Many boxes from Castile" and a large array of European artifacts were found by Narváez in Safety Harbor.
- The 1527 map identifies the latitude of Tampa Bay exactly, and gives the bay the name, "Bahia de Juan Ponce." There is no logical explanation for naming the bay after Juan Ponce de León other than to recognize it as the place of his colony and the place where he was mortally wounded.
- A chronicler of the 1539 De Soto expedition noted that their landing site just inside Tampa Bay was 30 miles west of the entrance to the "Bay of Juan Ponce." There is only one place in Florida where the entrance to a bay (Tampa Bay) is west of the entrance to yet another bay (Old Tampa Bay). This further defines the Bay of Juan Ponce as the "bay within a bay" that is now known as Old Tampa Bay.

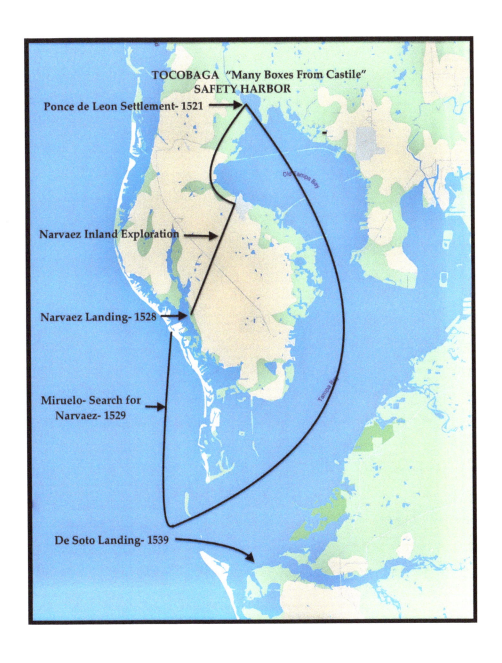

TOCOBAGA "Many Boxes From Castile"
SAFETY HARBOR

Ponce de Leon Settlement- 1521

Narvaez Inland Exploration

Narvaez Landing- 1528

Miruelo- Search for
Narvaez- 1529

De Soto Landing- 1539

About the Author

Jim MacDougald is a Florida researcher and historian. His years of study led to the 2018 publication, *The Pánfilo de Narváez Expedition of 1528.* Upon its completion, MacDougald continued his research, intrigued by the possibility that Narváez might have found the remnants of the Juan Ponce de León settlement site of 1521 when he had found numerous European artifacts and "many boxes from Castile" on an inland trip to today's Safety Harbor. Although it is known that Ponce de León had established the first colony in today's United States somewhere on the west coast of Florida, lasting from March to July of 1521, its location has been debated for centuries.

MacDougald's research led to the discovery that maps were, indeed, provided to Narváez, and that these maps identified Tampa Bay as the "Bay of Juan Ponce." After acquiring the very rare maps, MacDougald wrote *The Maps That Change Florida's History,* published in 2021. Intended primarily for scholars and serious researchers, it is highly detailed and footnoted, and focuses more on the maps than on the stories behind them. It provides compelling evidence that Narváez had maps, complete with accurate latitude scales, and completely revises the way that the Narváez expedition is seen, changing the dialog from one that makes Narváez and his advisors appear as incompetent fools, to one of understanding that they knew exactly what they were doing and handled the travails of the expedition as competently as one would today, given similar circumstances.

At the urging of Florida Humanities, MacDougald wrote *For God, Glory, and Gold* to tell the story of the early Spanish expeditions as he would tell it to a friend, free of footnotes, endnotes, references to research sources, or a lengthy bibliography. The references and bibliography are there, waiting for any serious inquiry as to the source of information that was utilized in the writing of this book, as are digitized versions of the 1527 and 1529 maps, which are available upon request. Inquiries are invited at jimm@wesven.com.

MacDougald resides in St. Petersburg, Florida and Beaver Creek, Colorado, with his equanimous wife, Suzanne.

Printed in the USA
CPSIA information can be obtained
at www.ICGtesting.com
LVHW050715210824
788845LV00001B/13